Reeling Backwards

Raymond Evans was born in industrial south-east Wales in 1944, a few months before the D-Day landings and migrated with his parents to Australia in 1948–49. He is best known as an Australian social historian, widely published in such fields as race relations, convict studies, war and society study, gender relations and popular culture. His writings include *Exclusion, Exploitation and Extermination*, *Loyalty and Disloyalty*, *The Red Flag Riots*, *Gender Relations in Australia*, *1901: Our Future's Past*, *Fighting Words*, *Radical Brisbane* and *A History of Queensland*. This volume is the third of a trilogy.

Also by Raymond Evans and published by Ginninderra Press
Half Century
The Merry Dance

Raymond Evans

Reeling Backwards

Poems of Reversal and Reflection

Dedicated, in fondest memory, to
Deborah Ann Bishop
(1962–2020)
of Edmonton, Alberta,
who loved music, the magical corners of existence, and me.

'You are meant to lose the people you love. How else would you know how important they are to you?'
F. Scott Fitzgerald, *The Curious Case of Benjamin Button*

Reeling Backwards: Poems of Reversal and Reflection
ISBN 978 1 76109 272 5
Copyright © text Raymond Evans 2022
Cover image: Jahara Rhiannon

First published 2022 by
Ginninderra Press
PO Box 3461 Port Adelaide 5015 Australia
www.ginninderrapress.com.au

Contents

Arena	7
Biograph: the Right Place	8
The Offering	12
Dropping In	14
Poem (Unclassified)	15
Before the War	17
History Lesson (2020)	18
Identikit	21
The Company You Keep	22
Solution	24
A New Day	25
Dance of Time	26
Breakfast	28
This Old House	31
Badland	34
Still Here	36
Bedfordshire	37
That Moment	38
In Praise of Isaac	39
Another Early Morn	40
Historian	42
Moreton Bay 1831	44
Virtual History	46
Cycles	48
Limitation	50
Wondering	53
Old Gold	55
Succubus	57
Moments (1999)	59
Escape	61
Retrospective	63

Midnight Torrent	66
Last Time for Everything	67
You Know the Way	69
Anamnesis	71
Tableau	73
Home and Away (1979)	74
Climate Change	77
Encounter	78
December 1967	80
One Night in Sixty-six	82
Fair Warning	88
Communion	89
7 Delungra Street	90
Surviving Graeme	92
Paradox	96
The Gates of Love	98
First Kiss	100
Boy (1950s)	102
December 1956	104
Out and About	106
Me – As Acrostic	108
Transported	109
Generation Gap	111
Getting My Religion	114
Old Friend	116
Birthday (3 April 1953)	120
Kidnapped	123
Fitting in	127
Garrison Town	132
My Nan (1977)	134
Be Sure I Know	139
Crossing Over	142

Arena

The stars take their seats
for the moon's horns,
once more,
to spear my heart.

They wink and nudge
each other,
fluttering their programmes
in the bristling wind.

And I,
like some capeless matador,
stand quietly agape,
awaiting a clean penetration.

Biograph: the Right Place

Born forty-four and feeling glad:
Nazis smashed at Stalingrad.

One year later – their defeat!
Dance with Mother in the street.

Forty-seven: Wintery fear.
Parents say, 'We're outta here!'

In forty-eight – no hesitation:
Join the global mass migration.

Six years old and on the prism,
encountering anti-Communism.

It's fifty-five and, as I play,
Bill Haley outsells Johnnie Ray.

Fifty-seven: adolescence –
Confusion, spots and wild tumescence.

Fifty-eight's portfolio:
Deftly dodging polio.

By nineteen-sixty, feeling blissed.
Me and Chubby do 'The Twist'.

In sixty-two as I've enrolled,
street action gains a new foothold.

Vietnam; conscription, back to back.
Beatles, Dylan face attack.

Then sixty-five, that protest year:
Start to probe the wild frontier.

A dancing fool through days hilarious.
Sixty-nine: Age of Aquarius.

Now everything is getting good:
Nineteen-seventy – parenthood!

Published work by seventy-one...
Social history has begun.

Moratoria; Apartheid;
Women's Rights: a bumpy ride.

Whitlam's sacking shakes the nation.
Exclusion...and Extermination.

London, Punk and racial riot:
Seventy-seven – never quiet.

As Brisbane coppers terrify,
Bjelke-Petersen riding high.

Workplace brawls; marital squalls.
Seventy-nine and Britain calls.

Working at the PRO.
Margaret Thatcher has to go!

By eighty-two this wonder child
admittedly now running wild.

Teaching students by the score,
writing of the Great World War.

Then back to London, workmanlike,
marching in the miners' strike.

Encountering every new obsession:
Arrested now for drug possession.

Eighty-seven: *Moonlight State* –
relishing Bjelke's fate.

Conflict history's now perennial,
even in the Bicentennial.

Red Flag Riots; Gender Studies;
debating academic buddies.

Popular culture makes its play,
barnstorming through the USA.

Workplace demands now all-consuming.
Marriage shaky; illness looming.

Mind and body – deep distress:
Six years in the wilderness.

Then somehow once again emerging.
Fighting Words with spirit surging.

New millennium: Towers falling.
Retirement soon becomes enthralling.

Queensland history so amazing:
deep research and crystal gazing.

Radical Brisbane; memoir too.
Poems arrive out of the blue.

Climate haywire; Fascists returning –
alone again through this downturning.

So many old companions gone.
Ranks are thinning. I beat on.

Sitting, writing, staying calm:
Lifeline fading on my palm.

So twenty-nineteen's not so cheery.
Whatever happened to Timothy Leary?

PS:
… And now the maw of 2020:
Masquerade…portents aplenty.

The Offering

Love, the guest, has come
with a heart-shaped stone
for your stone-shaped heart.

I would do better, undoubtedly,
skipping it out
across a lake of tears,
skimming it impressively away
before me,
than slipping it
into your pocket of spells,
your heart of stone.

I searched for it so long
upon a broken shore today:
cool and smooth to the touch,
an unremarkable grey,
size of a modest hatchling
in my hollowed palm.

Costing nothing but time
and really of so little use:
No blood to be got from it!

The bemused look
as you took it…

It may well have had
What is the Point?
inscribed on it,
like those gay
conversation sweets,
those Candy Hearts
we used to buy.

But cancelled now –
cancelled by time:
Lovehearts for Sweethearts,
reading, *LET'S GET BUSY;*
BE MINE! –
MARRIED IN WHITE/
YOU HAVE CHOSEN RIGHT
and the like.

And sweet to the taste,
unlike a grey pebble,
held inside the mouth
merely to allay thirst
for a time; or to deliver
a brief counterfeit to hunger.

Dropping In

The possum landing
on my porch
where I was standing
with my torch

Who made me jump
and then cry out
is but a plump
and friendly lout.

Poem (Unclassified)

Perhaps this poem
loiters with intent,
curled like a ringtail
in the stem of my pen.
(They can inhabit some
ridiculously small spaces,
you know!)

Or simply floats formless:
Words congealed in
captured ink,
amoebic – slouching towards
A4 to be born.

So I am sitting, pensively
considering this poem
in its guises –
as words released –
black words –
ready to run out
like black chickens
from an unlocked pen
across a wider expanse

or rising up,
a squabble of seagulls,
sensing some distant feast;

or maybe a sea eagle,
eager to soar
from a lighthouse tower
out over the main

or perhaps curled more
within the heart:
a snail, soft,
glutinous as an embryo

or a baby sparrow,
nested naked there,
almost ready to sing;
dancing from branch to branch
in a forest of wonder and guile.

Before the War

Three trees aslant
like sabre slashes
across an ashen sky;
flame trees, lean and thrusting
at the scurrying clouds.

Somewhere,
Kafka adjusts his clothing,
polishing down his hair.
Freud tosses in his sleep.
Josephine Baker dreams of
                    hot baths.
Matisse stifles a yawn.

The old days retreat
imperceptibly, shedding
                    their routine,
adjusting their margins.
Everyday people askance,
                    marshalled
down streets of gun-metal grey…

And skies like granite,
poised to crack.

History Lesson (2020)

Cook's *Endeavour*
with its bleary venereal crew
now scuppered, lies circumvented;
while the *Ruby Princess,* reputation bedraggled,
borders unprotected; impatient at Sydney Cove,
discharges her pestilence.

Yet no small pox this time…
Magnification writ large!
Bigger than Texas –
A rotund Red Menace,
rolling like tumbleweed
down abandoned highways
of our tenderest dreams.

This Great Big Virus,
looming over us
like the Great Big Climate Tax –
remember that one? –
(Not discounting, of course,
some other Big Things –
like Beheading Swords
bright across the media;
or Weapons of Mass Destruction,
coming soon to
a neighbourhood near you…)

Or that Great Big Bowling Ball,
once hurled across screens
to strike us, one and all,
down and out.

And I am of that dangerous age –
well within the target zone now –
able to recall
a time of hearing only 'AIDS!'
and of the Grim Reaper of '87,
grey-tattered and decayed…

The bowling alleys all now defunct;
yet, somehow, not us.

Recalling too
the tumbling Red Dominoes –
those Great Big Dominoes
that would crush us surely
if we did not pre-emptively crush and
'destroy the village in order to save it':
Ben Tre it was – a small city actually –
and four thousand other villages besides…

(At least,
that was the Theory…)

And now a Global Village apparently at stake
that fear mandates us to destroy;
to save or install, this time, something
seemingly to Big Pharma's gain
that we cannot,
in our masked panic
at the onslaught of numbers,
even, as yet, comprehend.

Identikit

Make no bones about it:

I am somewhere buried here
in the broken shards of me.
Just so as now you know.
Keep digging: you will see.

Anyhow, I'm pretty sure
I'm right here where I went;
although some bits have come
unstuck in all the merriment.

So, if you calmly salvage
this busted pottery,
you can manage to assemble
a fair facsimile

still gawking and fast-talking
with a brisk, distracted brain;
and stringing clues together
on a single mental skein

that only breaks, if break it must,
in the forests of recall,
where breadcrumbs dropped here
                          long ago
have blown off in the squall.

But if I just sit quietly
it all returns again
and I come alphabet-alert
in this fissured cask of skin.

The Company You Keep

Avid Reader, 2019

To my right,
Bukowski, Dickinson, Eliot.
At my left,
Heaney, James, Le Guin…

All set in place – amply mustered here:
a shelf of loquacity.
Intoxicated
and clipped enunciations:
Lodged in here
among the lightning spirits.

And the awkwardness
of me – some little black duck
amid falcons and swans:
Tiny dark spine
on display,
exposed to public view,
brazening it out,
far removed
from history's realm,
away over there
across the shop.

What purchase
have I here? What right?
Always but not quite
where I should be;
a little beyond
my uncertain capacity –
my unappointed spot.
Always punching a little
above a diminishing weight.

But, fuck it.
Please pull me out
nonetheless: note the sheen
of my covering.
Finger my creamy pages:
Do you read me?

Might you even select me
out of all these,
carrying me off
on your impatient path
to the next latte
and the ping of your phone.

Solution

After scaling mountainous volumes
towards misty peaks of knowledge,
always in transit,
never arriving with
any satisfaction of arrival,
I shoulder now only
this little bag of words,
a rucksack of necessities
for the journey.
They bounce and clack,
cool, smooth pebbles
in cabal against my back:
pebbles of modest shade
and a sombre cadence,
echoing all that is essential,
at last, to know.

A New Day

With your stories
a cellar of spiders
and your dreams
an attic of air,
you live at close quarters
with old cushions,
a tap that works
and an unmade bed.

You amble about:
A battalion of books,
like watching sentinel;
stairs a treadmill –
a growling pain in your knee.
Writing new poems now
on the backs of old drafts
and gas bills –
saving paper.

But, above you,
in the long bedroom,
Solomon Burke still calls,
Are you with me now?
Are you with me?
Crows on your veranda
are crunching eggshells;
and the trees, like green dancers,
prance about the old house,
their skirts high in a bracing wind.

Dance of Time

Such a night of it!
Stumbling upon 'The Wild One',
embalmed in an underground crypt…

Fell asleep around ten,
wondering on – of all things –
The Byng Boys Are Here
at the Alhambra:
Khaki audiences
and sweethearts,
lost in
If you were/
The only girl in the world…
away from the cordite and rats.

The bed this morning
an absurd tangle
as I kick and plunge
all night in the morgue and mud,
romping and humming to the music…

And waking today to
thoughts of Joe Strummer
and the 101ers'
'Key to Your Heart'

(Why this? Why them?)

Just an urgency
to hear that pounding:

An' I'll never be the same-same...

Parenthetic to an abrasive life,
punctuated by that percussion;
and a dilemma of choice,
circling always in my head,
of three short numbers,
curious and effective,
ever-changing,
to grace a gathering
I won't myself be fully attending,
in the event of my death.

Breakfast

Home Grown Honey,
'shining like a new diamond'
(but, of course, amber)
abuts the organic salt,
more herbal than mineral –
green head-piece
nonchalantly cocked.

Thrown together again,
bang against each other
on the crimson cloth,
like two old pals
comfortable in their intimacy
after another night on the tiles.

The pottery pig,
pink-finish scored
by the travail of years,
his open back anticipating
the symmetry of
another approaching egg,
stares off into the distance,
curlicue coiled primly
towards the honey jar.

The silver spoon
I only just wrested
from an over-zealous crow,
lazes elegantly
on the willow-pattern plate.

The petite teapot,
so Japanese and
intricately swirled
with a constellation
of blue-star blooms,
brims again
with Fire Starter tea,
sufficient for one:

oolong, ginger, rhodiola,
barberry, bark, cinnamon,
jasmine and star anise.

The crow – cheeky bastard –
is back for his eggshells,
his corner of quinoa toast;
perhaps a few mung beans,
a smear of tahini
as though the spoon incident
were of no further consequence.
Beak agape –
the familiar caw and cluck
thoughtfully modulated –
before stirring again,
spiralling upward
in a spectacle of blackness.

And so
another quiet day begins,
handcrafted with surmise:
the cicadas, a dependable static
as summer closes in;
the trees translucent;
pool limpid…
The towels are folded;
the driveway meticulously swept
as if proffering palpable welcome
to guests,
never appearing to materialise.

This Old House

Oh come visit me
in my household of words.
Present yourself on
my veranda of birds.

In the hallways of music,
avoid all the dust.
Brush down that old chair
if really you must.

This home endures here
for the heart, soul and mind.
So open your ears;
let your spirit unwind.

It pesters your eyes;
massages your brain.
Eschew every blemish.
Ignore every stain.

Hear the refrains of time.
Read the books of the past.
Reside in the moment.
Relax at long last.

Release all your laughter
and dance through the rooms.
Forget all the clutter.
Cold-shoulder the brooms.

Excuse all the peeling;
likewise all the cracks.
It's cemented with memory,
secured with flashbacks.

The fridge needs defrosting.
The pool pump is broken –
but what trouble we
with our consciousness woken.

It's spacious and cosy
and piled high with treasure.
No harsh judgements here
and no great displeasure.

There is only an archive
of every delight –
enduring temptations
for each appetite.

So stand in the doorway
and jive in the halls,
as legions of volumes
smile down from the walls.

There are pillows and cushions
and doonas and puff.
Grimy shelves groan with riches.
There is never enough.

And on nights cold and raining
as the wind howls about,
there is warmth here and welcome:
come in and chill out.

Badland

The camel in me
plods on toward
the oasis in me.
Will it drink from me
and rest today
in some renewing shade?

Or is this some
new mirage:
another shimmering
on my far horizon –
trick of the light,
signifying nothing?

I sit here silently.
A distant bird calls.
Short rushes of breeze
ruffling the greenery.
The murmur of traffic
away out there.

And I have nothing much to say,
hoping like a supplicant
for the unencountered to appear,
some smiling intervention.

*(Please do not pass me by again today.
Please astound me.)*

The camel in me,
stabled and enduring,
is thirsty for reward.
The oasis in me,
winking in the sunlight,
awaiting to be inhabited.

The various parts of me
all here, ready…
If only this desert round me
were less impervious;
and the sand less blistering
beneath these splayed, calloused feet.

Still Here

There are moments when
the morning blackbirds
almost capture
my chia toast

And my soft-boiled egg
runneth over.

There are moments when
I trespass again
the empty spaces
the little dogs left.
A ghostly thump
in this house
to my solar-plexus
as they leap for my lap.

There are moments when
I catch a sense
of you pausing,
passing the kitchen door
on your shadowed path
to the painting room.

These are the moments
when silences curl about me,
commanding consideration
in their confusion
of mockery and solace.

Bedfordshire

Up the wooden stairs,
mirror-image only for company.

The cat gone; the dogs long before.
And you, of course.

Do you know I still sleep
to my half of the bed?

Years later,
as if hoping in the night

the bus that once left me behind
might exhale to a stop –

a familiar stop
on the forever road.

The doors will open automatically
and you will all pile out,

as if returning from a special outing,
somewhat dishevelled,

tired but happy;
wiping off the sand…

And without waking me,
curl up routinely

all on your side
of the nothing-really-mattress,

beside the couldn't-chair-less.

That Moment

Tapping biro to thumbnail,
waiting for evocation:
something you once said to me…

How you were squatting
down, fixing your sandal,
squinting up
through a slat of sunlight,
falling on flaxen hair
to the open neck of your blouse.

Asking something so unexpected –
asking of a sudden,
What would you do if I left you?
Just like that – eight words.
And brought it all undone.

For right then I knew,
just as suddenly,
that, with no trouble at all,
concrete can turn to air;
aircraft fuel
can melt steel girders;
and that nothing signed
and delivered
is ever truly sealed.

In Praise of Isaac

All Hail Isaac!
What can't he do?
Captain of *The Snodger*
with his Bronco crew!

He rides the railways.
He reads the signs.
He knows all the ways
of Virgin Airlines.

And he's never afraid
to speak his mind…
This world would be a better place
if there were more of Isaac's kind.

I wrote this little impromptu verse in late 2019 for a very brave boy named Isaac Tilley, who was dying of a rare, depleting childhood illness. Isaac was obsessed with trains and aeroplanes in particular. His devoted Granddad was busily converting a Boonah cubbyhouse into a model space-ship called *The Snodger* for Isaac before his passing. The Broncos football team had agreed to attend its 'launch into space'. Sadly, however, Isaac did not live to pilot *The Snodger* as planned. His memory is preserved in the children's book, *Captain Isaac and His Snodger Space Ship*, which now helps to raise funds for medical research into childhood motor neurone disease.

Another Early Morn

Wind starting up.
Lizard runs for cover.
Crows diving for crust:
the interplay of this and that.

All quiet on every front.

Sipping chai tea
and thinking history:
Vietnam and the trenches,
outcry and riot –
the internal maelstrom
of then and now.

… That dream last night
of freeing refugees
(or were they slaves?)
Stubble on my face
turning to white.

(A cathedral burns.
A species dies.
I smell no smoke.
I hear no cries.)

The present, serene and silent.
A swirling Dervish past:
Guevara's death; the Paris Commune;
the poisonings at Kilcoy…

And the future's retreating back,
calling out over its shoulder,
Is there anything you need at the shop?

Historian

Heading for the morning meal,
a convict shackled at my heel.

Tahini on the quinoa toast.
Contemplating Logan's ghost.

Sip my mug of Morning Thunder:
Colonists engaged in plunder.

Crows partake of eggs and bread.
Queensland hides its frontier dead.

Basking in the early quiet:
Hey look! An anti-Chinese riot!

Lively music, just for kicks.
They're locking up the lunatics.

As I'm climbing in the shower
Labor Party comes to power.

Staring off in dislocation:
ongoing racial segregation.

All ready now to face the day:
Federation on display.

West End is the destination:
Considering all-White immigration.

Bus comes early, so I run.
Now they're rounding up 'The Hun'.

Meeting friends; lively discussions.
Next, they're turning on the Russians.

Attending acupuncture session:
Hold your hats! The Great Depression!

Afterwards at the Green Grocer.
Jap advances getting closer.

Then, to South Bank for a stroll:
sudden shock of rock'n'roll.

Whirl of restaurants and shops.
Bodgies taking on the cops.

Waiting at the transport station:
Anti-Vietnam demonstration.

Home again to ginger tea
Bjelke blues still bugging me.

Long day closes: crows are back
as Gough Whitlam gets the sack.

Thinking of my nice warm bed.
Hanson rears her ugly head.

Vegan dinner, furthermore:
refugees and Iraq War.

Climate crisis now extreme.
And so to bed, perchance to dream.

Moreton Bay 1831

for Ian Duffield

Sometimes I see them still,
their short hoes and scars.
The lattice of stigmata,
glistening tight
as they bend to the task.

I note emaciation:
the harshness of the light.
An instinctive cower as
constables and overseers pass.
The whips and clubs they bear.

I see the insolent tattoos
that comfort and entrap,
indelible on encrusted bodies:
matted hair; fouled costumes;
busted old shoes; naked feet.

The iron chains;
shackles rasping the shins.
Treadwheels slowly turning.
The Triangle in Queen Street.
The Gallows in Burnett Lane.

I hear them whimper in their sleep;
break silence; groan into the dark.
I do not see the horrors in their dreams,
the slash and cut
of the lash across their dreams.
The bloody gouts flying…

I see the hulking one,
chosen to flog for scant indulgence.
Soldiers standing about,
striding about in fine form.
Turrbal transfixed at the display.

A commandant on horseback

Stench of the place: meagre portions,
corn mash and gristle
dumped from dirty skips.
The captives' reddened, groping eyes;
their dysentery and delirium.

The hopeless, haunted eyes

And crouching behind bushes
then making off –
bashing off their fetters
in jungled overgrowth:
A dream of freedom and fair women.

Familiar food and home

I see them fording rivers,
squinting into the sun,
blinded by beach and ocean –
wretched in the green magnificence:
the terror and splendour of the place.
Growling bellies; defiant roars

and dark shapes circling in around them.

Virtual History

I write for the moonstruck,
the fabulists, the fools

for those still living in hope

that Cook's ship
will burn at Wahalumbaal

that the Castle Hill convicts
will take Port Jackson

that the Eureka rebels
will retain their flag

I write for the dreamers who dream

that Kelly's armour
proves impervious

that, at Battle Mountain,
the Kalkadoons will win

that no one fails
the Dictation Test

and for those who speculate

that the Anzacs will mutiny
at invading Turkey

that Phar Lap
returns from America

that Ern Malley
is the Real Deal

and, somehow

that Joh
fizzles out in gaol

that a thylacine will step
nonchalantly from the forest

and that nothing
will save the Governor-General.

Cycles

for Nick

As on through this life
the budding leaves,
the falling leaves:
Sweet green arrival
and every leave-taking,
the trees withstanding.

As down the seasons
of welcome and farewell,
the interludes of communion:
the holding and remembrance
of lore and love,
evergreen at mind and core.

The passing moments,
silent in the spaces of solitude:
rain steadily falling;
the slow tides running –
the heart inside
a ticking clock…

Bearing witness through time
to mighty births and tiny births –
deaths, births and deaths –
tiny deaths, mighty deaths,
cradled in pain and hope.

Pulses pound.
Heart fills and aches.
Spirits climb and fall:
pain arising; but joy returning.
The tears that come with all.

As around me here
my own past and
the past preceding,
stalking an eternal present,
the wider present,
broad and wild.

And the shadow of disarming futures,
descending like a juggernaut,
circling and teasing;
rain returning; night coming on.

Limitation

Were this poem a sand mandala,
it would be flooding down
through my fingers now;
not hesitantly
as these lines appear.

Its grains would land,
as through a funnel,
right on target:
its shades
and perfect patternings;
the soft gush of sound
as the sand descends.
Its form and subtle sense assured.

It would grow outward
from a tranquil heart
into its girded universe
in ripples of magenta,
turquoise and bone.

Sepia, maroon,
dijon and gold…

It would cascade
in amber and sandstone,
crimson and rose;
tinier ripples of
cobalt, denim and crepe;
sage, emerald and umber.
It would swirl outward
as days passed.
It would mesmerise:
its billion granules falling.
The hand so steady
with scraper and tube.

Eyes so skilled:
Each grain to its station.
Each colour to its regiment.
And people passing
would stop and marvel.
An admiring crowd would
surely gather round its rim.

And I would know exactly
where it was going,
assuredly along its plotted course –
unlike this poem,
flat, monochrome, linear,
edging gingerly out,
not running any gamuts,
creeping down
to the edge of the page.

Not circular and encompassing
or lavish in ornate grandeur;
just somehow existing here,
expecting to live alone
as some mendicant might,
awaiting salvation:
some respite of survival.

Rather than certain obliteration
in the smudge of a palm
or breaths of dismissal
back into a whorl of nothingness –
the deepening crevasse
of Time's raging river.

Wondering

What do I do when you come?
And I am standing
there among all the others,
craning down a sloping aisle,
heads bobbing up,
the untidy cavalcade coming out,
wearily seeking their hosts.

And you,
sharply now into view;
that glossy sheen of hair
unmistakable
and suddenly real to me.
Your singular outfit,
chosen so heedfully
for the big impression:
Long, slim legs,
the skilful cosmetics;
your grace of movement
carrying you forward
through your qualms…
that slight swagger of precision.

And this brash certainty, surely,
another coat of make-up.
Your body language – a study
in control and apprehension
as you move into slowed motion,
at last making me out.

And I, not moving –
just my mouth perhaps moving,
my arm coming up,
trying for a smile;
but no words,
just a certain look
as your face draws down.

And your mouth shyly
finding mine,
both saying nothing,
unfamiliar as yet;
and yet, in our certain ways
wantonly familiar.

Old Gold

Waking,
and you, golden beside me;
face half-crushed to the pillow,
mouth askew like
a broken rose.
The lambent sun kissing
the down of your cheek,
filaments shining –
a radiant ignition.
The rhythmic exclamation
of your small snores;
their modest exhalation,
all together here
in our careless room.

And the room itself now golden,
awash for a dawning moment
in mansions of sunlight;
remembering our evening
of plunging, creamy breakers,
tidal surges
and the locked momentum
of our ebb and flow,
our salty precision.
No one harmed
in the making of this night.
Laughter and cries
in the velvet dark;

and somewhere, far off,
Jackie Wilson singing
'To Be Loved'.

Lying here, scarcely moving
beside you,
within the grace of you;
and the scent of us still
a surrounding halo,
a lingering resplendence
uniting all the senses:
odour of jasmine;
serrations of sunshine;
the spell of your presence…

And the halting iridescence,
this new day, of time
upon the gold of our bodies.

Succubus

And then there were:

all those things she blithely said:
the words of solace on the bed.

The words of passion, fair enough;
but other words that called my bluff;

that raised the bar of expectation –
eliminating reservation.

There was this breeze. The curtains flapped.
I lay there still; my soul kidnapped.

The room was dark – obsidian night;
my tongue was tied; her eyes were bright.

She spoke of futures crystal clear,
of open hearts and plans sincere.

I swallowed every word she said,
my body limp; her white legs spread.

Her voice caressing in the dark.
Her fingers cool; her small birthmark.

Her words encouraging and near.
Her easy grace; her tongue in ear.

All calculated to seduce:
her heated breath; her running juice;

but more than this – sincerity
and promise got the drop on me.

I fell for her. I fell for it.
I fell and fell till ground I hit.

And all those statements of ardour
dissolved into a game *de jour;*

A passing fancy taking flight –
a running fugitive of night.

A jaw and face turned tight and hard.
The forearms crossed; the body barred.

And leaving me this stone of dread:
this hollowed home; this empty bed.

Moments (1999)

1. Evening

Green Papaya
and you as I watch:
first dinner
and you, young
and shining, discussing herbs
with the old assistant,
taking bright leaves
from her small, dark hand
against the olive wall;
everything translucent.

2. Midnight

The reiki, businesslike
on your cramped belly,
skirt down; and REM
night swimming through the dark;
hot tears on my fingers.
In the rain
at daybreak
we swim together,
world dancing.

3. Afternoon

Unearthing
the Malay's grave,
like detectives,
unmarked
in a rain-darkened cemetery.
That night
(Coleman Hawkins on the player)
together like bandits,
like panthers,
our bodies unhinged.

4. Morning

As we ride by
my old home
on a street quieter
than my mother's complaints,
a boy emerges,
running down the front steps.
As you leave,
you offer mother-of-pearl
washed by sea foam,
writing of the roll
and lull of the sea.

It is beautiful
what you write.

Escape

And so I am flying –
in the dream I am flying
and the clouds below
somewhere between
Turner and Constable:
rumpled white cambric,
bunched and scattered
with the stars above
blown into eddies,
whirlpools of light
(like Van Gogh's neon swirls)
and the moon immovable,
an ivory scythe, hanging upright
in the toolshed of night.

At first in the dream
there we were:
two forgotten warhorses
still yoked together,
pulling our familiar
gun carriage, paint peeling
off its sides,
faithfully through the grey mud
of some abandoned battlefield,
hostilities long over.
But we old horses do not know.

Then abruptly torn upward:
a sudden serration
of release from you,
side ripped open, weeping
from the shock of partition
(but no matter –
all wounds will heal)
and risen here on uplifting winds
into a billowing stratosphere
of renewal and uncertainty,
swooping and turning
playfully 'as in a gyre';
and marvelling at the ease
of flight and occasional acrobatics
in the chill caress of night
and the buoyant, transforming air.

Retrospective

We weathered in our time
earthquake and flood,
bushfire, hurricane.
Class struggle even
on our streets.

But we could not
survive each other.

That agonised night
you left,
I could not stand.
I could no longer read
and barely write.

All your letters:
disclosure and promise
on blue-ocean paper.
Still in their blue envelopes.

I am just writing,
you would say,
*to let you know
what you mean to me*

Hard now
cracking open
envelopes like
blue eggshells,

broken eggshells
of starlings and robins.

*We are both
pretty strange,*
you would say.
*We love so emotionally
and fight the same way —
boots and all...*

Harder now,
reading this at last:

*You know what I mean,
don't you?
With us
it is all or nothing...*

So now nothing,
tending still the blue pool.

But nonetheless

*Don't worry
about other people
splitting up.
We are not going
to let that happen to us.*

(Don't worry, darling.
Don't worry.)

*The best part
of our lives
is in front of us.*

Fragile pages of empty shell…

We did not cling
to an inglorious aftermath.
We did not cling,
she and I
(well, maybe just a while).

And, when the carnage ended,
the birds could return.

Midnight Torrent

Into darkness the sweep of rain –
no mere shower tonight –
the elemental thud and gush
down the tiles,
steady, then rising to battalion
                              strength
in its increase;
falling back temporarily
as in retreat,
then rallying, lifting
under a roistering wind,
rattling bare branches
like a conclave of staves,
minatory in the black air.

And the downpour,
slanting invisibly out,
an enfolding siege:
an onrush of heartbeats;
or heartbreak descending –
echoes of a soul's outburst
across an empty room,
expecting no comfort or address
save its own lavish release.
A capricious deluge,
masked by night,
anonymous in its excess,
demanding paramount ransom
                              and capitulation.

Last Time for Everything

Your carnival spirit,
dancing in
out of the sweet rain.

I had laid out –
do you remember? –
small chunks of carob;
nuts, slices of fruit.
But you moved past those.

Your scarlet dress,
the billowing one,
clung at the nipples,
up over your head
and off…

And the rain
out there interminable,
bashing on the tin,
percussive.

Nothing else in our ears,
eyes tight shut:
equal fish,
straining together

Wet as a mermaid,
scales sleek and cool,
flexing like a salmon,

twisting pink-tippled
under me

Heading unstoppably up,
up the downpour,
for requital and home.

You Know the Way

Into my bed you come
all dripping –
your breast an imperfect pearl
and hand, palm upward,
bent backwards to the pillow
as if for a reading;
fingers languid,
one nail broken.

So it transpires
on another afternoon,
music playing: LPs on rotation.
And desire, a red-ant run…
A tiny foray into the clavicle
and then skiving off –
a happy little slide
down the white ribs.

Never predictable
between you and me,
either digging deeper
or ascending into laughter.
But a promenade in unison
all the same; stopping to talk.
Minds engaged to wilder feats
than our bodies can muster.

And we weave new threads
into our shadowed tapestry,
sum total of our shameless selves;
as we match and raise
in loud communion
some newfangled repertoire:
Ever companionate
within our noisy transcendence.

Surely a sort of beneficence
hanging over this:
the comic spasming
we two mad clowns
again allow ourselves.

Anamnesis

When I recall the sweetest of days,
I see your car crossing the cement
below my unit; and the morning sun
cutting the sharpest designs down there.
And coming out to you with
Beach Music playing. And taking off.

As we rolled across the bridge
to the island, I caught and held on
for dear life to a swirl of joy within me.
We were laughing so painfully
and wisps of cloud,
like cobweb, trailing the wind.

Your hair was cabin-boy short
and we lay naked at the margins
of an empty beach on faded grass.
You were wet for entry under a cobalt sky
and I mounted without preliminary,
holding exposed roots of a cotton tree.

We perched on bar stools, ignoring
the patrons of a squalid pub,
drinking sangrita and grasshoppers,
still entirely stoned, as the Go-Gos
sang 'Our Lips Are Sealed' and
the room dipped and dimmed.

In the late afternoon, we found
that little place; only us,
sitting at rough benches
as golden sunlight across your tanned face
seeped through the greenery above,
and I saw how much I loved you.

They brought us, we said, the freshest fish
we ever tasted, direct off the boat;
and I spoke of the Aboriginal song
I had heard, just the day before
on the campus, of the Jindoobarrie
at Woorim, where we now sat:
their longhouses, their fishing praus…

But all gone, long since, I said.
And you wept.

Tableau

White light.
Black bird.
Deepest night.
Whispered word.

Lost boat.
Calm lake.
Hopes afloat.
Hearts ache.

Star gleams.
Water lapping.
Moonlight beams.
Dark wings flapping.

Home and Away (1979)

Along the miles
of ivory tiles
(where Londoners once
dodged Doodlebugs):
and I am back down here
within these cold aisles
before hitting daylight again
at Bank or Angel,
grimly up the grubby stairs.

The pull of bookshops
at Tottenham Court
on a drizzly day;
embraced eventually by
Dark They Were and Golden Eyed
or Ray's Jazz Shop near Soho:
The Fortean Times and Johnny Hodges.

Striding on,
assured in this city now,
no need for *A to Z*.
Uneven pavements and clatter;
the blank, impervious stares.
Re-entering a maze of tiny lanes,
crossing broad thoroughfares;
Trafalgar Square sloping away
in memory and dream.

Waking in Camden
in my attic bed.
There are ducks on the Lock.
Animal cries from the zoo…
Safe up a winding stairway;
snow briefly powdering
the slanted windows
that Christmas morning.

A tiny machine
plays rhythm and blues,
tracks meshing together,
formidable in this confinement;
and I am undisturbed here
alongside E.P. Thompson,
Orlando Patterson: flush with ideas,
plotting new forays
over *Time Out*,
writing compulsively home
of my forensic itineraries.

Trudging back,
aware of Australian forests,
jarrah and kauri,
beneath these streets;
past purple mohawks
around the station.

Striped scarf on tight,
holding tighter to briefcase
and the Indian takeaway.
A Naïve badge on
my herringbone coat,
attracting nothing.

On up Primrose Hill,
through a chill twilight,
the little shops closing;
sequestered and alone,
feigning insouciance,
twisting the key in my pocket
and banking on
an envelope or two
on the antique table
in the vestibule.

Climate Change

The kisses fall
between the lines:
Only the mouths dancing
in the white ballroom.
Time evades their moment.
The umbrella stays folded.
The tramcar awaits.
They are caught
in a snowstorm
that binds their lips,
sears the tongue.
They are not cold.
Their bodies pulse, aflame.
All else is frozen.

Encounter

Portuguese words
in a tequila of night;
castanets and piñata
in drunken moonlight.

Her hair black and slickened.
Her eyes flash with fire.
Her breasts are half-offered.
Our brains are haywire.

We sit at the roadside.
We pass round the salt.
We share the same lemon.
We share a gestalt.

We share the same pavement.
The cement is warm.
Our touch a magnetic,
electrical storm.

Her feet they are naked.
Her nails they are blue.
Her demeanour grows languid:
her breath honey dew.

We lie in the gutter,
examine the stars.
Our thighs press together:
two sleek avatars.

We're emboldened and subtle.
Our words slowly dance.
It seems I am crossing
some massive expanse.

I reach for her fingers.
I'm drifting away.
The music we're hearing
is Sidney Bechet.

We know we are lovers
preceding embrace:
These two beings breathing
in one breathing space.

In this Portuguese night,
our tequila of words
hover whirring above us
like two hummingbirds.

December 1967

Holt's exodus
keeps interrupting the Tennis.
Christmas again in the offing:
Swimming underwater
at Centenary Pool,
openly reading *Another Country*
Uncle George smuggled in;
lying in the sun,
tanning like suede.

*God gathers them
all up at Christmas,*
Mother intones.
Just you watch now!
She keeps tabs:
Otis Redding and
all of the Bar-Keys last week,
nosediving into that lake…
The Cowardly Lion;
the guy who wrote
'Twist and Shout'…

And so, as years pass,
recruiting Darwin
as a clincher
into her perennial repertoire:

the smallest of cyclones
and yet so many dead –
all because of Christmas!

She may have a point,
we concede.

Just then
a Christmas beetle
barges in:
its aureate splendour
disrupting her thesis,
spinning on the Laminex,
tiny legs revelling,
all in a whirr
in the season to be jolly.

One Night in Sixty-six

I see us gathered
on the cool asphalt –
the pavement facing the Hall,
vigilant for truth
in the midst of lies:
a silver cord connecting
us all: *Friends will arrive.*
Friends will disappear –
All in a hubbub,
sustained by laughter;
part-eviscerated already
in anticipation.

It is just the same old street,
the same old story
in dowdy Brisbane.
But we cross in flamboyance,
a little tide of beads,
scarves and rollnecks
this autumn night:
my natty reefer jacket;
Frank's Hasselblad;
Heather's platinum hair;
Terry, Les and Rose
charged by the currents
of each other:
ghost electricity, one might say.

*(But what should we expect
merely of him?
Surely tonight we cannot
expect too much?)*

Have I eaten yet?
Apart from cappuccino and No-Doz,
have I not eaten?
This crisp April day
already defying expectation:
About thirty, cunningly
evading cops,
marching in from the outskirts –
Bowen Hills to the City.

Ragged strips of cloud –
Beatson, McQueen and Laver;
Parr, Cleary, Summy and others,
all along Queen Street
through midday traffic,
lunch crowds baulking
at our rude signs:
No Vietnam Conscripts.
Stepping out like a streetwalker,
focused straight ahead,
cars honking; drivers yelling;
jaywalking towards Anzac Square
into the arms of the law.

Was I Chaplin,
Keystoned at noon?
Am I Warhol here tonight?

Perhaps just Holden,
alert for *phonies;*
or maybe Candide,
hopeful for miracles;
aware already that
Haley, O'Keefe and Penniman
have triumphed
in the bear pit of this place;
that Seeger, Robeson
and Lennon have all
preceded this night:
the Twist, the Stomp and the Riot…

He is so sparse up there,
so unsteady, perched
like a cormorant on
his high stool –
his guitar slipping…
(What is he on?)
His cadaverous frame
in its herringbone
suit; his face invalid-white.

This town could blow him away.
Snuff out his spotlight
on that bleak stage.
But his harmonica plays,
unlocking us, skeleton-wise;
and that flinty voice,
its acrid bite
gnawing into our darkness.

Yet this is prelude
as we all suspect –
The blank stage now
littered with cords and wires
and his motley crew,
buckskin and booted,
corduroy red/powder blue –
a discord of tuning up
and the yells beginning.
(They are incapable here
of a Judas call)
but they lob their bitter muck
nevertheless, shaming us all
who have recently known
the Beatles assailed
in this hopeless town.

And his boys,
like gladiators now,
silver-slicing the air,
advancing on the lip
of the stage…
(as we just marched?)
And he is
assaulting a piano,
mounting it almost,
no longer liable
but demonic in attack
on Mr Jones and Jones
and Jones out there,
still erupting in dumb fury.

We are somehow there
with him in our darkened row,
riding exultantly upon this
tense empowerment –
knowing, amidst a disciplined
cacophony, we are the exception here,
yet braced in our moment
anyway, praying this conquest
will be our future.

And the music – not folk,
not rock, but all music
right now, meeting on
a tidal shore, immerses us.
In these splendid minutes –
the alchemy of him and us and them,
Bob Dylan and the Hawks –
an alchemy of splendour:
trees bursting into bloom,
into flame,
the stage alight.
(Yes Brisbane: how does it feel?)
catcallers leaving.

An imperishable gift
for us, so unexpected;
and us, not worthy,
not ready by a long shot,
nonetheless standing now,
cheering like lunatics,
heirs tonight
to a light come suddenly shining:
this abrupt albatross
of transfigurement,
high flying in.

Fair Warning

'By God, you do persist!

If you ever parade me
in front of your friends
at high tea
like THAT again,
I swear I will loudly complain
the sandwiches scream
when I bite them;
and the teapot
is waving its trunk at me.

So forget about
my eating out of your hand:
Not happening – not for a second.
Be warned:
I am the Cannibal King –
the Bone Cruncher!
the Marrow Muncher!
I even bite
my own fingernails.'

Communion

We lie in shocking positions
on the sable bed.

But, with eyes closed, we could be
back on the mountain top
above St John's Wood.

The bare, flat rocks
spread like an altar,
trimmed with verdigris.

And no witnesses
but the forest growth
to our lank nakedness.

The awkwardness of you
on your white back.
Stone mattress rasping my knees.

I saw you in full
and unabashed that day
in raw sunlight.

Your eyes were pinned;
mouth uncontrollable. I put my ear
to the growl in your throat.

A tiny black beetle upturned,
nimble legs waving,
held my immediate focus.
And the sprawl of your hair,
spilling out, raven-wild,
upon the rank and trembling earth.

7 Delungra Street

for Trevor

On the tram back into town,
and you whistling into
your State High hat:
the old drunk,
leaning in to me,
cocking his head:
The cunt's a clown,
he earnestly said.

There were your
mother's peach balls;
and uproars of mirth
from a room
somewhere or other
in that whimsical house –
no need for peacocks
on the roof –
Del Shannon coming
loud off a transistor
left to its own devices;
and everyone about
their business,
glancing preoccupied
off each other.

Zooming around in the rain,
perfectly miming
'Blue Moon' by the Marcels,
tires in shrill harmony;
jagged hole in your Zephyr's floor –
slick asphalt
careening away beneath our feet.
Off to find damsels
in distress or fits of laughter.
The absurdity of everything,
budding like passionfruit
in the drizzle.

Time lavishly bestowed.
Silver in our pockets,
knowing the best burgers
and movie lines;
astounded by our wealth
of possibility
and its easy negotiation;
blindsided by nothing
but the onrush of our days;
and the unseen moments
waiting in ambush
like junkyard dogs.

Surviving Graeme

for Graeme Kearney

Graeme, in memories of you
it is all motion –
the maniacal way you'd drive
for one thing, back then,
hitting speed bumps at speed,
flying up into the air;
veering erratically off
the Cabarita trail,
ploughing with me
into that sandhill;
almost overturning
and leaving the road,
a tyre bursting,
breakneck down Mt Coot-tha,
balanced a while
over a little precipice…

But always laughing;
and if not laughing, singing
as we travelled –
God knows why –
to all those backblock
country shows
across the open Downs,
sun blazing,
the widest horizons of
blues and greens before us;

no car radios for help back then
but singing every O'Keefe song
by heart, on top of our lungs
as you banged away
at the steering wheel,
keeping time;
or driving all that way
out to Clontarf,
just to hear Rufus Thomas,
'Walking the Dog'
on that deserted café jukebox,
over and over
as we sipped our Cokes.
It was worth the petrol,
you would always say.

And you, at parties,
always a blur of motion
before conking unpredictably,
instantaneously comatose.
Just a whirr of wisecracks,
flailing arms,
all jig and hustle, bawling out
'The Gone Gone Song'
as though at
some last-throw audition
to cement
that elusive show business career;

or roping me into a duo
of 'I'm a Hog for You',
channelling Screaming Lord Sutch;
holding the room
in fits and awe –
a mesmerism of machine-gun repartee,
audacious and boundaryless,
amazing them and me,
though I knew you so well.

Our birthdays, ten days apart.
And we met portentously
that first school concert
night in forty-nine,
when I was a pussycat
and you were a tree
and I tried to climb you,
impressing you greatly;
as our mothers, little noticing,
chatted away that warm evening,
mine in her broad Welsh
and yours,
her slow Australian drawl.

It was a long trip, my friend,
going by so fast,
fuelled by drink, flirtations
and tomfoolery –
all those private jokes, touch phrases
and musical immersions.

You were always ten days behind
I know; but you caught me
off guard nonetheless.
I never expected
that swift departure,
far away up there,
out along the Strand
for a slow beach stroll;

because, Graeme, I was always the eldest,
and somehow you passed me by:
you caught up and passed

and you *never* strolled.
And you always hated the beach:
Your dry skin, so readily damaged,
matching your dry wit from
a perpetually dry throat,
and your taste for never leaving
a dry eye in the house.

Paradox

Now listen here Boyo,
my father would say,
No chaps out of Wales
can ever be gay.

It just isn't in them.
They're not so inclined.
They're too decent and wholesome.
They're too clean of mind.

So, as a real outcome,
it does not compute:
the Welsh are your real men.
They're not bloody fruit!

He'd sit back and watch
as his words took their toll;
while, positioned behind him,
Mam's blue eyes would roll.

She'd settle in yearly
for the Gay Mardi Gras
as he'd take himself downstairs
and sit in the car.

He never discovered –
this deluded fellow –
he was directly related
to Ivor Novello

who's now widely regarded
as the Welsh uber-gay,
who pioneered high camp:
music, stage and screenplay.

Born Cowbridge Road, Cardiff,
the 'compleat' extrovert:
gathers lovers like lilacs –
a 'consummate flirt'.

At Littlewood Green,
with his 'naughty' commune,
cavorts round in spangles;
sleeps with Siegfried Sassoon.

Is the toast of the season.
Is bathed in champagne.
Writes Hollywood movies:
Me Tarzan – You Jane!

He squires Noel Coward
and works with Hitchcock.
Keep(s) the Home Fires Burning.
Fashions brilliance from schlock.

With my old dad, his nephew,
supremely unknowing
of his famous Welsh uncle,
shining, starring and glowing.

The Gates of Love

The Gates of Love
have golden gables;
but rust adorns
the hinges
of the Gates of Love.

The Gates of Love
are never latched;
and many carve
their names
into the Gates of Love.

The Gates of Love
seem so colossal;
yet children clamber
easily over
the Gates of Love.

The Gates of Love
were garden gates
of deep crimson.
My father once painted
those Gates of Love.

The Gates of Love
led the way
to the House of Shelter
that lay beyond
the Gates of Love.

The Gates of Love
were cheap and common:
fading in sun and rain,
as years rolled over
the Gates of Love.

And the Gates of Love
swung wide
for all who came
and never seemed to notice
the Gates of Love.

First Kiss

Stomach clenched throughout the day.
Desire grew hot
with thoughts risqué.
But will my nose get in the way?

Sitting outside our café;
my mind in
utter disarray:
What if my nose gets in the way?

Oh, let the chips fall where they may!
The night is dark.
The branches sway…
But *will* my nose get in the way?

I'm hoping we can meet halfway.
Her eyes are bright.
Our fingers stray.
Don't let this nose get in the way!

Our evening seems one grand cliché.
This surely now can't
go astray; unless…
this nose gets in the way.

The landscape forms a rich bouquet.
My heart swells
like a baked soufflé:
the nose can*not* get in the way!

We move as though in some ballet.
My lips send
their communiqué:
'Nose! Do *not* get in the way!'

Our mouths now meet: it's all OK!
Her breath is sweet.
I feel blasé.
And *nothing* can get in our way.

Boy (1950s)

Quick! Touch wood! we always said,
grabbing for each other's head
as ambulances pass.

Swapping comics under houses:
Keep those hands out of your trousers!
Feeling bold as brass.

Eating several liquorice straps;
gun full of exploding caps –
nose pressed to the glass.

Addicted to the radio,
singing every song I know:
rhythms of first class.

Then the weekly matinee,
laughing loud at Danny Kaye,
sipping on my sarse.

At every corner, flip a coin:
follow where crossroads enjoin:
ignore signs of trespass.

Collecting cow dung by the sack
as the magpies plan attack.
Landing on my arse.

Working hard for pocket money.
Really trying to be funny –
often sounding crass.

Mispronouncing 'rendezvous'.
Hope the moon might soon turn blue,
stretched out on the grass.

Thinking Aborigines spent.
Wondering *where they must of went?*
Reaching an impasse.

Impulses and appetite:
moments crammed with wild delight.
Other moments sparse.

The Goons and tunes of rock'n'roll;
Toad and Badger; Rat and Mole:
Life – a radiant farce.

December 1956

for Harvey Collins

There were never strawberries
like the ones we had
that sultry afternoon
sitting on the step…
The cicadas so loud
the sound became the taste
and the taste, the sound.

And your mother, calling us
through the back door
for something else from the shop –
a lizard, poking
its head through
the long cement crack.

We were enveloped, weren't we?
We were cushioned –
so casually loved in those days.
Time bobbed and floated.
We could almost touch
its slowed motion;
and the fairest sun
kissing our small limbs.

… Silkworm hatchery or
ant farm, Harvey?
What will it be?

I was at home here,
the warm wood
coddling my thighs,
stamp album on my lap,
showing you my Penny Black
as the holidays began.

That big, blue-green house;
and, from a tiny kitchen radio,
the Chords sang,
Sh-Boom!:

Hey nonny ding-dong,
A-lingally-lingally-ling…
Life could be a dream.
Life could be a dream,
Sweetheart.

The first four lines of this poem are 'found' – borrowed from the lovely poem 'Strawberries' by Edwin Morgan.

Out and About

Sunlight freckles in
through pebbled glass
and, as I wake,
outside it is green again,
edging to brown.

Sky above as usual
brazenly blue and deepening.

So later, perhaps,
patrolling the day,
we can lie and watch clouds
turning to shreds and clumps –
or rolling off in their wombat herds.

Tadpoles impatient in pools;
and butterflies as we pass,
in black and white or technicolour,
dip and sway.

Around us
emerald grasses
grow on and up
in a buzz of heat.

And we are, in turn,
elevated and calmed
by this infusion
from morning's bounty.

And blessed in our brash boyhood,
with little grasp of gratitude
for warm soil;
the largesse of ancient roots,
poking through ground;
or that bird over there,
serenading; but keeping its distance
as we rove and ramble,
unawares, into our beckoning hours.

Me – As Acrostic

Running fast
And never tiring.
Young legs pumping.
Mad spirits pacing me
On paths of joy.
Nothing to stop me
Diving into this day.

Long hours before me:
Every expectation met.
Silver sheen of dew;
Light breezes ruffling thick grasses.
Intensity bubbling within me,
Entertaining myself with song.

Ever straight and never
Veering from my path
As birds watch in wonder,
Nestled high above me,
Sweetly heralding my advance.

Transported

for Graham Webb

Don't run! You'll fall!
my mother calls.

And so we run,
dogs yelping like Valkyrie
up ahead,
doubling back,
circling our tiny legs;
familiar houses a blur
yet all acute:
Power in our pounding feet,
the world ajar
and hot breaths regulated –
sweet breaths and
the pounding in our heads.

We can go on endlessly like this.
We need never stop
till lunchtime.
We have our legs beneath us –
the reckless legs
of a stampeding herd
the rustlers cannot tame.
We are the bandits on horseback.
We are the Mongol horde,
ready to make history,
today or tomorrow,
now the holidays are here.

So it is written:
we will gallop on,
marbles jumping in our pockets.
Our muscles are strong –
no need for bikes or billycarts.
We are foot soldiers
on bivouac,
arriving in a panting pack,
us and the dogs,
armed with soft-drink bottles
from the dump
for conversion to bullseyes
at the shop.

Then off again
without a word,
shoulder to shoulder:
mouths engaged,
chests abreast,
calibrated together
forever this way
along dirt roads and bush tracks
unwinding before us.
A relay team,
all rushing on as one
with our baton of youth,
into the mad, blazing adventure.

Generation Gap

Clouds fix into shape:
pale scoops and dollops
this windless day,
frozen in memory.

In the bullet-grey tram
upon olive-scalloped seats,
wending our way into town.
My chin to the window ledge,
feeling its rattle
into the bone.

But hardly your speeding bullet.

Just meandering along
and rolling with idle deliberation
and many halts
along its silvered trail.
The occasional uplift
of spark and whine
as it rounds another bend.

So today
it is Danny Kaye
at the St James
and then the predictable treat:
crowding the ice cream counter
by Penny's door
down the street.

I am – as may be anticipated –
some three rows back
in the slow progress forward
amid a clamour for service.
Almost all children
in this rabble today;
but one old man –
(A Digger? A Pensioner? A Tramp?),
in a coat that once fitted,
is buying his penny vanilla cone.

Just another moment
like the long tram ride,
the unmoving clouds…
But he is shaking.
Cone trembling
in his erratic hand,
gingerly exiting the congestion
with his modest prize.

And, in a final moment
as I watch,
the unsteady hold
betrays an eager mouth,
lips already parting to the taste,
as the small scoop
of solace falls –
It judders free,
tumbles white to the floor.

In that forlorn instant,
no one else noticing,
our eyes briefly lock – no smile,
only shock and shame
in a communion
of dismay;
as my uncertain youth
meets an old man's teary deflation –
confounded – with nothing
to offer as condolence.

Not even the warm penny
I still hold in my hand.

Getting My Religion

When I first met God –
not yet considered 'Dead' –
He lectured me: *Love not the World.*
That can't be right! I said.

God was old and wrinkling.
His hair as white as snow:
a broken halo round a head
that beamed a waxen glow.

God wore black and, round His neck,
a collar starched and white.
A leaden cross was hanging down.
His eyes were like midnight.

He sat with little children
caught up in His embrace.
I offered no encouragement
to His cherubic face.

I resented God: He took away
my Sunday morning shows
to worship Him at Sunday school.
We almost came to blows.

But then the Troubadours arrived
at our local Bowman Park,
with their panel vans, accordions
and stories of the Ark.

We sang of Eagle Wings that grow
from waiting on the Lord,
whenever fears are mountain-high
and everything abhorred.

We sang and sang – the Webbs and I –
these happy, hopeful songs:
Hoarse Throats of the Apocalypse –
the four of us in thongs.

We rode the vans to Rainworth,
to the off-white People's Church:
for fellowship teas; and, from overseas,
missionaries in long, prim skirts

Who warned of Communism
in firm, decisive tones.
Then more accordions, a double bass
and electric xylophones...

They warned of Chinese forces,
their faces cruel as sin:
*Will you deny Our Saviour
when that door gets broken in?*

It really was a hard one.
I was not entirely sure;
especially when Charles Darwin
wrestled Jesus to the floor.

Old Friend

Monstera deliciosa,
like captured dragon,
darker than moss,
peer out
through spiked railings
at the Gardens.

And my Nan,
caught there
behind the kiosk counter,
plays sleight of hand
with the coinage,
handing out
creaming soda and sweets,
while handing back
all the silver
in perfectly faked transaction.

I sit by the large enclosure,
avoiding the monkey cages
with their acrid tang
of piss and spoilt fruit;
the desperate bits
of wet, broken bread –
and the funk of sad inmates,
capuchin and baboon,
baring their red bottoms
to a gaping crowd.

And stare instead through the wire
at kangaroo and emu,
'Our National Symbols',
pacing a bare, baked
exercise yard –
wallabies flopping down
in dust and heat;
the odd cassowary;
some incongruous deer,
all concentrated
upon this moonscape of earth.

And, lumbering up
to the chain mail beside me,
like the museum's *Mephisto,*
dignified and painstaking
in its slowed motion,
this massive tortoise.
With each grandiose step,
a grey, armoured somnambulist,
ponderous now over
the thin mint of grass
I slide through the mesh,
before tugging it gently in,
chewing it deliberatively.

It is our private ritual,
the big terrapin and I:
This simple communion
of proffer and receive
each time we meet.

Many decades on I learn
we are both migrants here –
she from the Galapagos
where the hand of Darwin –
(Charles Darwin, that is,
pottering along that beach) –
plucked her up
one morning in 1835.

How she had then sailed
with scientists and crew
for years on *The Beagle,*
transported here at last
by its master, Captain Wickham,
just after the convicts left…

And watching then,
with her leisurely, discerning eye,
aeons of passing antiquities –
the ambit of many yesterdays
encased in that carapace:
numbers growing;
fashions, fortunes changing –
the evolution of it all.
The whirr and boredom
of life sentence
to her arid domain.

And then, myself as that boy,
determinedly inquisitive
but usually beaten back
by the prevailing torpor –
soon resigned
to a place devoid of history
and as parched of consequence
as that bald arena…

Yet holding on,
ever on the lookout, nonetheless,
to chance upon some mystery –
some hint of an elusive past –
even somehow to touch it,
without ever grasping
the shape that history took;
or how interminably
it may have been corralled.

Birthday (3 April 1953)

The morning is shining
and at last I am nine.

Tadpoles splash
in brown pools by our gate;
lantana glittering after rain.
New asphalt pungent
along the road; and, at the crossing,
water so luminous,
pearling over slate flagstones.
A tumult of morning glories,
hanging radiant from the cliff face –
a curtain of blue sapphire.

Above me,
the dappling branches;
and the old lady,
bending again to her roses.
Up ahead,
the eager corgi,
running to the diamond wire
for her daily caress,
the sun on our shoulders.

Flowering vines
somehow today more lovely –
the hanging leaves;
snapdragons, petunias and pansies
out along Atthow Avenue;

and these cloud formations,
bleached and humped,
like billowing sheets on the line;
or crumpled eiderdown
from some inviting bed –
fair-weather clouds today –
one now almost kookaburra-shaped…

And, on open display
upon a white paling
as I pass,
two lime grasshoppers,
sizeable and grandly engrossed,
happily mating.

At school, no one knows
it is my day:
we revisit 'Lead Kindly Light'
for correct intonation;
and the Gypsy girl and I,
her skin like cinnamon,
trade Chinese burns silently
under the desk;
as young Bill Hardcastle,
on a chair again,
spitting enthusiasm,
gives us by heart
'The Man From Ironbark'.

And walking home,
an Enid Blyton omnibus
in my school bag –
darker clouds gathering,
grumbles of thunder; rain holding off;
hoping my Merthyr parcel
has arrived today,
as in the best of stories;
and that, at least,
Mam, as promised,
has made her devil's food cake,
with the nine candles –
or perhaps her famous trifle –
for after tea tonight.

Kidnapped

That shard of rubied glass,
glinting a tiny fire –
roughly heart-shaped, serrated,
she had shown me:
It is my blood,
she solemnly stated.

She was different from the rest.

So…the Sunday school picnic
in Jones's paddock
below Mt Coot-tha…

Fancying myself
victorious in the sprint,
coming in last.
Awarded peremptorily
as consolation,
a bright red pencil
and metal cap.

Not so fussed right now
on all these Anglicans –
retreating to the creek's edge
alone; until an abrupt grab
from behind.

Although their kidnap is gentle,
held energetically on my back,
nevertheless, by a light-fingered two;
while she (of the serrated heart),
hair wild (though formerly plaited)
and tawny skin,
becoming so elated,
issues her orders.

Sun in my eyes,
soft laughter washing round me,
sprightly but tame in my struggle;
for all the world
the perfect captive,
enjoying their hands.

Take off his glasses!
She leans in close:
*Can you **see** with them off?*
So much glee
at my dilatory obedience,
my happy compliance…

She kicks off her shoes
and wades out,
tucking her dress
high above her thighs.

Then her shadow
over me again,
her conspirators now silent,
still holding on.

Her bare foot is raised
and the pink sole
caresses my face –
the pad so wet, toes pointed:
tracing gracefully, slowly
down my cheek,
cold across my forehead.

And so suddenly
it is just us –
eyes caught, her down-gazing –
that mysterious smile,
dusky haunches apparent,
foot moving assuredly, leisurely –
such astonishing confidence:
the urchin beauty of her.

Later, glasses retrieved
(though somewhat askew);
heart back
from climbing my ribs,
walking home alone
down Simpson's Road,
proceeding distractedly…

At our gate, my father,
mixing concrete,
looks up and smiles:
So you're home. How did it go?
(in his usual Welsh way).

I wander in.

My fine red pencil
has lost its silver cap.

Fitting in

First bite of a cherry;
Auntie May's old radio
plays Sunday morning hits;
bougainvillea arching above me;
Moreton sandhills, heaped and dazzling –
blinding white pyramids
against cobalt blue;
our buoyant, roaring creek
in the January wet –
and how red the bottlebrush,
the poinsettia…

From the day we arrived,
Cole's Funny Picture Books
failed to enthral.
And so too pee-the-beds,
stinking Rogers, Vegemite
and cockroaches.
Hating mosquitoes;
indifferent to raucous birds
or the taste of pawpaw.
Scared of mopokes.
Recoiling from witchetty grubs.
Baffled by bananas.
Openly opposed to watermelon.

It felt at first
an exile – the sinking solitariness;
the ruts and dust,
mudflats and mangroves.
Limp hanging leaves;
lantana and wait-a-whiles
clearly hostile.
Listless faces:
The same sad jokes,
belittling others,
told and laughed at
over and over.

Desolate.

We looked out
for things to love. We truly did.

Even the nightly insect circus,
spinning and whirring
on the red Laminex –
a crowded table rink.
The acrobats and skaters
so minute and intense.
Dad reading aloud
Oliver Twist
as they dance their tarantella.

Then at school,
the day we raked the hay.
Included abruptly
in their laughter
as we ran and rolled
into the warm, golden stacks.

And again,
that perfect night
I must now describe
as we sat, cross-legged
on the polished floor
for cartoons and Chaplin
on a makeshift screen,
before the towering tree.

Our wild mirth
eclipsing cicadas and frogs;
a gift for all beneath;
feeling utterly encompassed
at last by those around me;
as above, almost to the ceiling,
the dark-skinned girl
suddenly there,
her tiny, starched dress,
Rinso-white; wand in hand.

Her tinselled hair,
silver-lined in the half-light:
a glimmering angel above us
as we rose and sang –
all eyes upon her –
a surprise for our parents:

*Every little girl
would like to be
the fairy on the Christmas tree…*

And they all clapped.

And, on the day we left,
how they marshalled us –
the three old teachers
of that infants school:
Buckley, Mathems and Hussock.
We were still so small
as they attended us one by one;
a modest offering and
the shock of their arms around me;
each, in turn,
holding us to them,
startling tears on their cheeks –
these austere women,
normally so contained,
voices caught incoherent
in the moment of our parting.

And realising, in that moment,
their love for us;
and, as a final epiphany,
arriving almost too late
as I left those grounds,
our love for them.

Garrison Town

Nearing Christmas,
unlike the ones
they used to know,
the boys of air force base
gather round
a flatpack
from the States,
stopping work
at Eagle Farm
as the shiny shellac
spins
on the old gramophone,
hearing Crosby
so far from home;
and – first time for them –
'White Christmas'.

Bending forward
as children listen;
tears in their eyes –
most of them –
when he starts to whistle;
this Christmas
in the tropics
where no treetops glisten
in nineteen forty-two.

And so,
as Christmases come and go,
a ship finally turns in the river.

Up on Victoria Bridge,
a small throng,
all Brisbane-ites gathered,
maybe two hundred strong.
Not used to public singing
or drawing attention;
but all singing anyhow,
as occasion warrants,
'We'll Meet Again' –
doing their best
this sunny day.
Not sounding like Vera Lynn
or even Crosby –
not by a long shot –
nowhere near as good…

But, as I say,
giving it their all;
and, as they sing,
the boys, all holding ranks
down below,
are again beginning to cry.

My Nan (1977)

Old as the century,
barely arthritic
all of a sudden,
is a nanny goat,
nimble up the broken slope,
urging me on,
pulling at the looping grass,
to the grimy window.

Climb up now!
Look through yer.

The bare ward,
cold and still
in the undergrowth.
Enamel bed frames,
standing about,
turning to yellow.

That bed there, Raymond.
Where you were born.

And I am back on location:
The old infirmary of
the Merthyr workhouse.
(How many times have I returned?)

My mother, four days
in labour with little help,
only that frightened girl
backing off,
running off back then –
and no luxury of a doctor's visit
in such straightened times.

Every day
I brought her broth.

My skull is cramped
and wedged in a barrel,
fashioned to a point
like an artillery shell.
From my left cheek,
a lavish blood blister
hangs like a tonsil.
I know the story well,
recalling none of it,
reliving it fleetingly
each birthday.

Arriving,
already defaced:
fragile package,
broken in the post.

The ancient bed like a rack,
metallic; forbidding…

She brings me to this portal
on a blustery day:
a world more familiar
to her now than this dismal
December afternoon,
skirting these antique lanes
where Dad walked me; places
we'd shop; where Granddad
fell in the High Street.

Then up beside a freeway
with convoys thundering by:

Where are you now?

Yelling triumphantly in my ear
above the din.

I am lost is
where I am –
air thick with diesel fumes;
raggedy patches of weed
lifting sooty stems.
No one stops here –
hardly room to stand.
A giant billboard,
offering a contented baby milk,
looms above.

*This was Court Street
where you all lived –
The Labour Club across the road.*

Cliff face of grey stone
washed by inclement weather;
a mass indestructible:
houses uniformly windowed,
on up the rising hill,
sculpted, it would seem,
from solid rock –
long gone.

The black-skinned men
trudging home from the mine.
Wives making hot dinners
in back-room sculleries.
No one singing cowboy songs
in an upstairs bedroom now.
No one dancing downstairs
to the BBC.
When the house burned down,
three people died.

Our two silhouettes,
suspended in the smoke and grime:
Nan and I
just standing,
catching strains of
some old Merthyr lament
above the diesel roar;

fainter echoes of singing men
and a smell of home cooking
in the encircling gloom:
a trace still of cheerily making-do;
and the street orators
coming out again
to a hint of contention and snow.

Be Sure I Know

How to boogaloo down Broadbeach
and how to tie my shoe;
how to Stomp the Tumbarumba
and play the old kazoo.

I've hung around this staid old town
and scoured the state's south-east.
I know the ways of cap and gown –
stroked the belly of the beast.

You do not live like Dorian Gray
or even Nancy Drew
and be averse to show your face
or really have a clue.

So every day I have my say
upon a shining screen.
While few respond or even care,
I maintain the full routine.

I saw the birth of rock'n'roll.
I rambled through the ruck.
We rarely did what we were told.
We did not give a fuck.

I listened to Bob Dylan.
I smoked pot that same day.
I danced with girls and held their eyes
in every dim café.

I marched against each vicious war,
supported human rights.
I stood with Whitlam, furthermore,
against the parasites.

I wrote about the frontier.
I wrote of the Great War.
I wrote of men and women:
of lepers, crooks and law.

I wrote of hidden places;
of shameful, ugly scenes.
I rarely wrote of *sweeping plains*.
I entered the ravines.

I lectured to the doubtful.
I copped a lot of flak.
They did not know my quaking heart.
I donned the armband black.

I linked arms with my comrades,
so few and far between.
We battled on against the tides
of national routine.

I kept faith with those comrades.
We gave and gained support.
We fought against denial
in the land of false report.

So that is what I'm doing here
in my own redundant way:
still poking thorns into your sides
in this wild and grim ballet.

Crossing Over

One of those translucent days,
innocent of danger.
Skies blue enough for diving in.
Air slicing like a razor.

Yeats to his tower.
Thomas with pencil stub.
The Man from Porlock
tapping at another door.

Out here yet again –
no presentiment of peril
on my green, plastic chair,
breeze lifting the page,
vaguely cheery at this volley
                    of words.

As Brooke to the Greek Isles
or Keats to the Spanish Stair;
Shelley sailing to Livorno;
Byron to his swamp…

Or Owen,
crossing the Sambre-Oise Canal,
sniffing a brace of cordite
at War's end.

As with each confounding day,
sailing breezily on,
conflating, as usual,
the River Styx with the Rubicon.

May I die while running;
as I ran as a child.

www.ingramcontent.com/pod-product-compliance
Lightning Source LLC
Chambersburg PA
CBHW070911080526
44589CB00013B/1257